Molly Smyth was born in Belfast in 1931, raised in Liverpool and lived in London for most of her working life. She returned to Liverpool and died on Merseyside in 2014.

W0007764

North End Shore

Molly Smyth

Co Loa Media

First published 2017 by Co Loa Media

Co Loa Media
Cheltenham
GLOS
GL52 2DA

ISBN: 978 0 9928962 4 9

Designed and typeset by iKraal, Cape Town SA
Printed and bound by CPI Group (UK) Ltd, Croydon,
CR0 4YY

For Ginny Smyth (née Murphy)

There was no sign
that anything had ended
and nothing to instruct me
to forget

Elizabeth Jennings
Growing points (1975) Carcanet Press

CONTENTS

Annie

We stand with her remains
sworn at by the ferry
she'd lie awaiting trains
if she knew our fear
dismiss concerns levied
say take holy cheer
thank the deliverer
neither disturbed nor worried
by morphine driver's whirr
more a silk worm still
prayer from a yellow monastery
a promise my people thrill
the manner of her contained
Ireland accepts in tributary
once fired as rain
kids of a country's pain
proud at the morning jetty
her migrant sayings
like apples from Kilkenny.

Abira

Do you measure distance
looking down a bottle of beer
as if polishing chrystal
the tenor of your bones
a river wash them clear
time to be explored
the cormorants we saw rise
and cry in broken fear
last winter before the tide
will your lover have to lie
somewhere close to tears
if you say you'll try
knees and face at the sofa
a trapeze of wasted years
eyes trying to fix a place
where she records each instance
your faded artists gear
her presence mysterious fusion
does silver cup *her* ears?

Aurora

There's times I wish
I'd never been born
on this tired bridge
my taxi is gone
now leave me alone
to this third interregnum
what made me think
I was doing
getting jealous of drink
swallowing eau de cologne
Spring coming on
standing by the road
then the cloud breaks
a ship's coming home
cars weave like snakes
they see me walk
a bespoke sojourn
tell other souls
I'm not alone.

Azira

Why beseech another
set afire wooden frames
still our way home
cotton, gold and spices
what games we play
oars splice the breaches
sunlight runs with drums
we return the hail
these islands of summer
to settle here or fly
roam away from this place
a seething grass of lies
leave port in flames
inscribing with our whips
names on bloodied waves
forget don't smother
teach or join in praise
a cache of lovers
who ring our grave.

Alicia

Do we think of others
while screaming down the phone
the cross beams of mothers'
prayers for all those
whose thoughts are blown
down summer's blue river
drumbeats on marshy grasslands
museums where we walk alone
men flit like swallows
days throng with lovers
we can only atone
by water and evening sunset
sisters' looking for happiness
Guggenheim, Tate or Prado
playing cards with Velasquez
his hand like any other
more than we can know
I mean, does his light trouble us
quieten our tones?

Aleysha

I shift in a lemon light
say everything is all right
my lover wakes uptight
sunrise over Alexandria
where Cavafy lived and died
as good a vista as Thessinger
in Arab clothes faces tight
an iron kettle on the fire
with Bedouin across empty sight
salt drives a global warning
swallows thrum the dawn sky
her dance and drumming
from last night's fight
and last night's wine
will we see a Caliphate
spring an early surprise
tugs on the river ply
shining brown barges by
lips echo our delight.

Anneka

The *poetes maudit*
you always loved
keep me in the garden
is that all there is
beside your son
who goes back to him
the one who scatters easy
the fruits of women
day fades uneasy
salt claims an early due
is this just a dry run
for your evening blues
'I ache for a baby' you moan
what have you begun
to dance with northern rollers
dicey laughter jolted kisses
birds at dusk settle and hum
is it just by listening
water runs.

Adara

Who removes the cast
do only kids look askance
at the long grass
Verde across the terrace
Campari, dark glasses, slap
a city from its fast
The Café du Repas
I pray at the border with France
and regret the chasm
loving other women
shielded from your glance
who am I to damn you
whisky colours thrum and sing
sea birds arc and prance
in summer of their circling
weigh again at last
the doubt fire of your glance
Verlaine from your past
rhythm of such balance.

Bella

Men who want women
eat calf's liver and greens
something clings to them
in the coming night scene
wind hush soul freeze
they fear their dreams
worried what they might see
the city's muffled seethe
a drumming dry wheeze
hope ladies might please
drink drink every evening
face white hotels like death
breath bitter as almonds
leave what love has gleaned
sanctify what is left
between golden fingers
they see what Goya's seen
richer, older, needing water
wine, bread, falling leaves.

Banya

Trees of a green oasis
that freedom always boosts
Susa loaded with freighters
gentle winds on the Karasu
a banshee boat for losers
it will slay your mood
your lies and protestations
your cries for food
wine's dissipation
a raw supply of senses
shattered workers pool
their liquid defences
it's hard to explain
what you've been through
so why now start shaking
camels piss at stations
hrummp and wait for crew
on yellow sand slaking
don't let love betray you.

Beattie

When love is only
three missed trains
your face is solace lonely
was is it only a wish to share
that love should stay
instead of slipping at the bar
those lines going nowhere
the wine we gave away
to nights of ached for care
outside the café window
trees in the gentle rain
cigarettes show your sins
wrap them around your heart
you'll never change
in rooms near a car park
my mother used to scold me
you still rush by today
stations of your litany
we drank to stay sane.

Byrony

You stamp at an instant
cry in a broken field
whisper resistance
will you drown down here
by cliff top trees
your ravaged visage
luminous as the moon
hold your knees
in search of soothing
why do you say
tough men are easy
pitted as cloying clay
you came back sister
is your life a movie
a cure for limits
Nicholas Mary Imperious
say Mass to receive
hope on wooden pallet
send it to the sea.

Billie

Don't talk to me and pause
give me one of those sighs
I've heard those tales before
it's my home if you realise
not your own interesting life
make out how you tried
when you waved good bye
you left me barely alive
all you said then denied
Piyuli, Manous, Matta Grosso
how you spread your lies
and you expect me to follow
where this story ends
about the way you cried
me on my iron bed
a lonely beach feeling sore
bottles, tar, wondering why
you coursed away due north
carried on the tide.

Baya

The ice cold Diva
makes no sense to me
when she sings *Ave Maria*
your face tragic as the sea
a poem makes me sleep
dream what has been
in circumstances of our own
can we ever make history
each morning disowned
like love we gave to nights
to seamen and Cafés
stunned beneath the lights
your laugh a delight
like sunshine on the breeze
a taste of paradise
but no one scolds easy
or owns their own scene
praying only for *Bollinger*
you were so released.

Catherine

We dream of justice
defeated, tossed away
dream of a love insistent
do we think of Solomon
who never sought that reign
what were we thinking of
who will excuse our insolence
our trawled remains
as slaves or prisoners
calendars say time
needs only one page
to know cruel pain
uncertain questions
lie unborn everyday
a hurt bequested
cigarettes smoked at the instant
drunk we had our say
time fritters like the spirit
our burning flame.

Clara

You stroll off the meter
but you don't see me
dressed for cashmere theatre
blow upon polished fingers
at the Salon du Té
and whisper with policemen
discuss suitable places to meet
sip Darjeeling
there's no need to kneel
protection now guaranteed
stands like a bushel of wheat
it whispers *Blondie*
but what of those times
you danced by the sea
and sang out your rhymes
did crashing waves greet you
did you see me in rayon
waiting by the street
remember our screams.

Carrie

You'd gamble anything
your daughter says
including unforgiven light
around your blue eyes
could you ever retain
the time she prized
chasing you like a pain
the times she cried
falling snow or rain
letting go as you came in
do you see her that way
smoking your Capstan
maybe you can smile now
laugh each St Patrick's day
but who dissolves love
unhooks the gas ring
lets blue flame rage
dogged by such things
is no one to blame?

Cresta

Standing by the beach
she says don't leave me
the only crying is the sea
can anyone retain
that unforgiving need
broken sesame's
I see her tears and I cry easy
what do you want me to be
she shrugs at destiny
dunes shift in the evening light
in her eyes a gimlet steel
she says 'you'll bleed'
I walk in uncertain hue
how to enjoy freedom
when emotions turn blue
a life of dull marriage
always needs
its summer retreats
the could have been.

Diana

Great swollen days
without your care
make no sense to me
yes, go on, watch me dance
you know about mares
but you've never made beds
you smoke without ask
drink *fino* from a chair
under a broad brimmed hat
a white faced *dinero*, dark glasses
you breathe thin air
shout *mas vino*, *tapitas*, clap
are my legs your delicacy
this snail of an affair
music releases me
I wonder if your blasphemy
is lost without prayer
like being raised
no love to spare!!!

Dany

The weekend sings
when no one comes near me
especially silent things
I fall between their shadow
can't anyone see
how much they wallow
in the yellow light of Spring
is this their dream of the sea
wages paid like Disney
a safety net coastline
beyond the cherry trees
do they set the time
lines of the petrol station
smell of diesel on my jeans
my best blue Monday
forget bonus schemes
take holidays on Tuesday
enjoy sweet freedom
fuck authority.

Dee

Am pretty sure of what to do
around your knees
a tattered sheepskin to warm you
when birds cling the ferry
passion doesn't crease me
I never took you or holiday
your lover nor your son
you say I'm not easy
well, what's done is done
interesting but uncaring
you'd never fight for me
water can't bring yearning
what is said might not be true
when orange fires the breeze
I'm not thinking of you
this night of coming blues
Merlot arrives from Sainsbury's
drunk *en famille* but crude
ghosts set free.

Delilah

You laugh like Camus
but it's not the heat
deserts don't frighten you
you'd say that fools
always miss the beat
when looking at ruins
you are like an almond
brown and seventeen
before the wind
will you blow away
like their leaves
nothing to harm your stay
just the yellow and grey
poverty of hurt dreams
poems on hot spring days
inside you hum a tune
turn your head at screams
ignore the blues
your spirit sinks deep.

Ella

Was I worth a light at Faro
green evening stripes the trees
smell of sardines from boats
and the raging kitchen
I smell the rain and sea
warm beneath beam fittings
where you eat alone
I brought you tea
you said with words of stone
don't try to clone
another happier being
I don't turn you on
she wants to dance and sing
but her opacity
splits me like a tangerine
cuts me to the bone
above my frayed dungarees
birds from Africa fly home
will she ever see?

Elsa

Are there consistent issues
that deny my need
or does other tissue
hang off skeletons
with lip sticky greed
and glorious friezes
standing by the beach
who says let her be
just out of reach
not particularly frugal
with their solidarity
but I hear coins jingle
a manifest delicious
dancing to my creed
between shore and distance
salty tears continue
your eyes out at sea
shell shocked beings
lie around your feet.

Eva

Can you love me
your eyes like fireflies
the way she sings
look at me, I whisper
they dance like satyrs
what do you think
can I do it with you
two bottles gone by
this Sunday in summer
this side of the river
a thousand nights
I spent with her
strung out on methadone
what are *you* like
jangling like a drone
will you still be
here to wonder why
this side of the sea
too pole axed to cry.

Elanova

Dancers are ill at ease
with spiritual gain
it molests their poise
the ladies, the women
she feels their technical gaze
sweating like an oven
Our Lady holds the beam
on cold lit Sundays
no matter what they sing
her Ma all scorn
is lost within her ways
what she adores
they'll invite her along
chant without praise
their love and songs
on trips to the sea
she won't wear grey
or find ways to agree
love without shame.

Freya

The scimitar of hope
splices lovely days
chimes out my freedom
I'll go home soon
in a sun that frays
poor yellow stone
down New York alley ways
I see the moon
the Five and Dime, Macey's
the cool evening light
when debt gets paid
no one's surprised
do my parents know
how I pray
indifferent stars unfold
clouds shaped like domes
my quota of praise
I'm made to atone
the glory of my gains.

Fara

She hates the dull why
the pleadings for freedom
in sought after light
but what is she doing
making chocolate maxima
pasting yellow windmills
mulling over wine
fire turns her seasons
she will be fine
night boils her thoughts
afternoons her reason
it slakes her days frozen
who brings a clock
to the walls of this prison
when you know the knock
the kids will continue
regular as the heating
lilac as the evening
their faces wry
beneath moon's steeple
to chant without crying
a time of leaving.

Frederica

Your tunes still weave
patterns on shimmering trees
notes from a blue island
add them to my shipwreck
a pirate roving sea
golden confessions
on swollen straits
I kick my heels
down guttered alleyways
can't feel my knees
but I still see dreams
you cried too easy
before a mast one Sunday
bread, wine victory
torn netting wood and sail
your privateer schemes
billow before me
like a broken creed
your howl is pity.

Falecia

What's up with dreaming
and loving the sea
do horizons redeem us
like luck or a number
brighten our features
when love's struck dumb
there is still the time
for you to seize it
don't wait for a tide
take too much sun
find a reason
to have some fun
bring gentle forgiveness
splash and believe
moments are a pittance
water rolls for everything
waves surround your feet
don't be done believing
fine green evenings.

Frinka

Fumbled steps at evening
heart beats like cocaine
skipped Atlantic breezes
at times a summer whistle
by some hunted door frame
a drumming racket twisted
a wish, more than any trip
how different is your game
have I missed that ship
the scent of your perfume
arriving from the station
laughter from every room
your fame in café places
a portal serenade
when you see the faces
come home lady
arrive like any freighter
don't rake me with your blame
whisper gentle names.

Greta

Who will tend our bones
listening to the rain
does a river run alone
let our song ring
on early trains
birds we heard sing
cormorants that soared
we maybe see again
mud cakes their claws
their cry on broken wires
those September days
diving before the tide
stuff we swore we'd never do
when we count the gains
wonder if that's still true
struggling by the sea alone
could we find a way
to drain a summer phesemnone
find a place to stay.

Georgina

What keeps you moving
a crescent moon at Easter
a sail that fits a groove
an arc of scurried waves
why you want to flee
do they know your trade
your flight to water
by troubled season
by map or distant slaughter
while you keep the morning star
and look to the sea
consider us from afar
your love of freedom
guarantees no sweetness
a plank of sky to dance on
you sing of truth
this island's a prison
fire the Caribbean
lace your pirate's linen.

Gavrila

Who's your next mate
my lover asks me
I shudder at an empty space
I'm sat here thinking
can't you trace
the orbit of my feeling
her thoughts are churning
at such infidelity
but dance away again
freedom is not for givers
living by the sea
looking down the river
what I have to explain
let her know subtly
the sky has changed
see that one with braces
I point along the beach
she never leaves a trace
'You' she screeches.

Gabriella

Should you ought to spit
in this house of spirits
Oceans dance your lips
let them engage or quit
take me to my limit
make that tourniquet twist
be like someone else
my bones in bits
all love sealed in chests
find hope at every instant
escape on pirate ships
cry in middle distance
bolstered by the tide
make laughter visible
let happiness decide
spend every fighting minute
tender as a glimmer
the moon a gentle silhouette
not yet risked.

Hannah

Paintings are my scene
museums have a lonely grace
hearing screams
I stare out of canvas
that's really my fame
the world my caravan
from summer nights
or gas fired winter places
how often do I lie
heaven for you to look upon
the scent of my face
you are like M Duchamp
who before me rushes
buttered names on graves
his Fountain flushes
unshaven waiters wheel
cognac to my place
oranges and dreams
my oiled face.

Hermana

She knows what's been around
an unbroken sky
leaves a naked mound
a rose broken sleep
when others are high
she makes her great leap
a kid from 'Rica not New York
she promises to lie
with a thousand women
although born and weaned
and raised by signs
a kid from yellow fields
now she dances in the towns
city lights pure delight
away from farming sounds
but her country, country grounds
still demands reasons why
home and little ones
her eyes don't lie.

Heba

On methadone you never say
ordinary is too late for me
there is always a train
a thought gone half past eight
that could be eternity
making you find ways to pay
stations or runways
don't affect me really
my cool and burning rage
barbiturates are not the same
when you look out and see
faces on the highway
they say it needs work
just do it steadily
but I won't jump and jerk
or care who prays
budge or shift my cold feet
no one can state
where I need to be.

Holly

My own breakfast test
feel a lover's trauma
don't I feel blessed
sailing as we speak
with a raging lymphoma
all her troubles leak
howl like the wind
complaints amorphous
a drowning sound
that sinks like lead
a real performance
pictures in my head
jukebox in the kitchen
everything roars
seek wine at 8 am
like she's never had rest
chocolate with toast
tomorrow more tests
act the holy one.

Hera

If it's children and dogs
just be what you are
by warm lazy logs
if that's what you want
from the river Alt
sea weed in your font
but help me realise
what's going on
in someone else's dreams
close to here
pictures bear a lonely scar
for all my needs
dancing on egg shells
fires everywhere marked
by your iron bell
roses pant in fog
bring me what she can't
but no more loss
beneath a fallen star.

Honesta

Sometimes you can't explain
the hurt you feel inside
the way her face fails
nothing in the way
but retreating light
or how her eyes play
my lover, proud, unbowed
no longer hails the sky
but dances in the clouds
once she jumped the rail
found places safe to lie
plenty of times the jail
a woman of love and rage
she beat out her time
but did not cap the flame
what's the game
behind my confessional sighs
her face blue as rain
did I ask why?

Irene

What if the stars are great
my daughter slowly fades
lonely and in pain
doesn't matter what drugs she takes
the walls are still grey
in her cell she hesitates
listens to the clock
on yellow wing what's to say
her phone is still blocked
her kids have done screaming
confined within their days
lilac as their weeping
they see the creep of moon
watch time roll away
I've seen them happy
laugh on school evenings
since she's been away
but they visit 5 and eight
and each night pray.

Illustria

Here's something for you
you think you come first
with all your places to go
you're not enough born
to rage against thirst
when summer gets torn
the sea still surrounds you
have you time for mirth
home's not a clue
by book or by 'phone
your trail well versed
to know you'll be going
will you try this evening
drive away swearing
pass a naked café
salt and stars like glue
where all debt is burst
your eyes dead blue
hung easy air.

Idell

Who do you want to suffer more
me or your blessed lover
outside the Café Du Bourse
it's a perfect sunny evening
kids looked after by mothers
is your love done by keeping
as if you know better
in life between the covers
to get rid of evidence
you think you're clever
wiser than the others
in the cotton jet set
Ray Bans on the terrace
September withers
another burning furnace
drink whisky with a soda
evening's cocktail colour
a breeze blows from somewhere
will you close the shutters?

Isabella

In days of autumn fire
night rides black and cold
stars come out like ice
no matter what desire
the wind is fierce and bold
it knows each gleaming lie
the love of dreaming
if we're not at home
a flame across the sea
our love falls in the mire
on mobile 'phones
no lack of *rire*
how you replace fear
tells us we're not alone,
no matter who conspires
in the yellow night
you appear atoned
a name for every try
written on a board.

Iba

Don't make a fuss
she carries yellow lists
do not try to purge
or rail against her fits
your heart against the system
a place by her breasts
if you to want to learn
be prepared for this
simply do what she returns
or go and find the road
drag or get a grip
knowledge never comes alone
guide the pain like tamoxifen
keep the middle distance
ride another rill
or leave for somewhere else
in this house of whispers
the sea is not your guest
a horizon for your trip.

Ilana

The wind blows bad breath
across our fences
who cares what caress
it stirs in lighted cellars
what cast as we bend
flowers to the mad jealous
bad armed drunks who jar us
encourage shy friends
like tickets to the rush
across our coffin lands
nothing sensitive
in their brutal stance
will anyone want us
dressed to fend
their heavy advances
or carry by naked tread
our indebtedness
to the inventive West
mourn our death?

Irena

She hears a strange whisper
the sound of a removal van
and thinks my sisters!!!
each move the last trip
no one faults her tan
every tune moves her lips
she wears a wooden cross
the bars are full of men
especially by the goods yards
they rise like ghosts to greet her
she walks home with them
each sea green evening
but barefoot prays alone
her dance done
she'd rather have a home
rather than the whistle
of another drum
she was never this driven
but who gives a damn?

Joanie

With your love of Horse
a needling wire
it brings no justice
the offerings of Jesus
your ice cold fish knife
cuts our morning smile
the tide is never easy
how different midnight
on burdens we carry
our demons ride home
on phosphorous signs
but who needs to moan
at ourselves or scream
when love breaks the line
or friends play mean
we sail off course
our situation dire
a methadone remorse
a lightning fire.

Juna

As if to dissect me
the wind soothes the lime
and cypress trees
on hills beyond the ships
a metropolitan light
screams, forget her lips
I drink red wine
curse in stumbled night
against the blue skyline
a young silken woman
with her lover swine
moves closer to the music
the drift of a Du Wah song
beats a gentle whine
smokes like blue marijuana
notes wash the scene
my future on the line
a table of broken roses
no reason why.

Jayleen

We stood by unlit lamps
a tree, a bridge, shaking
waiting like tramps
for kindness to share
red lips white faced
cigarettes without care
listening to that song
wine sipped and champagne
who needs to belong
the cleave of crowded bars
cargo ships and freighters
rooms with dark marks
we can be happy here
watching the rain
tack down station cafés
you would not hear me
say straighten up our game
ask how much we pay
shuffle our remains.

Jana

2003 wasn't finished with me
not after that screening
my partner Sandra G
the photographer of breasts
unashamed melanoma dreams
is up for a festival
what should have been
dazzling different by the sea
has to fit her chemotherapy
howling down the 'phone
raging in midstream
she shouts through her bones
poets don't die intestate
swept away like leaves
sometimes they dance and stay
knowing how I feel
she turns away wheeling
laughs at my screams
whistles at the ladies.

Jolee

Smoking a cigarette
a lover's old face appears
fulsome not lonely yet
geese rise and sail
haunt the sky like deer
I knew her in jail
a snow blanket around me
she always cheered
ice blue as the sea
colours of the Argentine
not anyone could go near
where she had been
absorb uncertain dread
that brought her here
a place safe to tread
a woman who wouldn't let
flame cross fear
shared jokes and bets
then disappeared.

Kara

The corridor deadly blue
her smiles don't show
what your ancestors refuse
strangled by swaying steps
she'll hurt you with her no
that dancing smile at rest
is she looking for the chance
to take your tales and show
the sorrowed lands of distance
a knife wound to the sea
a young woman free to bestow
love to a midnight dream
the engine screaming
descending by mountain furrow
is she still scheming
to warm her toes
ferment desire
a place without shadows
around your fire.

Karen

You'd gamble on anything
your friends say
including the Easter calendar
I wonder kissing your lips
watching cormorants in the bay
roll into harbour like ships
did you think of her then
salt and perfume not far away
cleaning their wings in wind
did you think of us then
smoking or kneeling to pray
going out as you came in
smiling for other lovers
what an image they make
songs drift one to another
was your life a fake
a search for nights delayed
where winds blow thin
ashes off your grave.

Katya

Do you want me like this
love isn't forever she hisses
you don't need to make a fuss
powdered lightly she emerges
a shadow of light insists
the fragrance of cold purges
others play at lovers
twelve days a body twisted
its epiphany not yet over
she is betrayed at every turn
Catherine Villanova my sister
I am your distant curse
a courtesan at every court
mandolins cannot help persist
your scourge of tort
nor poets chant their lists
no ship unfurl sail
before your gifts
of storm's entrails.

Kalaya

You used to write to me then
of furs and feathers and winters
an injured fighting pen
bloodied in a tenement
you wrote of smoothing kisses
sybarites of Harben or Tashkent
Fulton Street summers
dollars, beds, your fancy business
beneath seething Brooklyn
you work in the five and ten
leave me in splinters
I'm not going home again
to that wee drug retreat
the poor and lonely resisters
laying down eighth street
why only help the *tethered*
you my rootless sister
donning boots and leathers
snarling like a Bittern.

Kathy

Absolved of troubles
I've wrapped in time
she passes beyond my look
uncertainty arrested
how we're still alive
my tears flow ingested
delivery, testimony, manifesto
between us down the line
love hangs by leaden pennant
believe me a life is shared
by one decision of that Tontine
a broken woman, a new year
they tell me 'see reason'
a rattle of gates by chime
cannot shift our history
nothing disturbs the rubble
or accepts our decline
our poverty a bubble
we sometimes refine.

Laney

She sees the creep of moon
regular as the easy night
rise all too soon
fish on Friday beaches
the kids who drink wine
from yellow glasses
men who want women
to give meaning to life
someone who likes living
she twists a boat smile
lemon sun blinds
the decks of July sunshine
but the goal, the ball
she has a mind
to leave this shore
she laughs and croons
what makes her frightened
takes another route
a tune she lightens.

Leona

She follows a trail I've sown
the wind blows over
wrapped around like a gown
pulled from dull marriage
she is passed between others
her face a carriage
deduced by jail or sentence
she bites quilted lovers
sunshine somewhere dances
she was / you are/ I am born
a kid from yellow troubles
who practices her scorn
on a ship or by a star
that a candle can't smother
a miracle of smaller parts
don't burn down walls
we're not here to suffer
love's slow on the corners
this great blue morning.

Lara

Who wants to be free
says my lover
I do, she lifts her hand easy
nothing between her and the sea
the breeze is kind on the peninsula
don't you want to succeed
her bright horizon
not given just to anyone
her toenails crimson
bright colours of her lipstick
she thinks she's a fun one
the wine caresses me
with hopes of eternity
she says no one's told her
God knows where she's been
it's a short step to clarity
the notes are all in order
marriage carries harmony
a symphony forever.

Lacey May

In a spartan café
redeemed from the sea
let me trade
a blonde or wispy marriage
for a coming enemy
shadows make merry
in the falling rain
saddened at the infirmary
echo of empty cradle
doctor's sad visage
more than we can ever be
love gone by barren carriage
down hospital alleyways
the absence of heartbeat
sounds a dismal train
on St Anthony's quay
loss brings no certainty
just whistles away
at sorrow again.

Leila

The turn of stupid days
scourge her great freedom
a river estuary
the streets and diners
awaken a sense of ease
solace out of crazy
not a real home stay
walk these yellow streets
gaze of Madam Du Prey
where all debts get paid
beneath cool trees
blue drinks hang on trays
Our Lady holds her navel
in the cold light seasons
whenever luck strays
no matter the law says
the river still needs
across broken seas
sisters from other cities.

Maria

When did I start crying
was it going back to Ireland
or when my son asked why
Nana loved the horses
you who poured sand
on that first recourse
on the ferry, kids playing
is that why I was cursed
anchored or in chains
you say my Ma is a slave
a martyr to her pain
I laugh a venerable grace
you the kid's daddy confess
you've run aground
can stand it even less
all this sighing
stop acting like my Ma
in troubled dust and dying
he can't be bothered.

Molly

Could you love me
you think you dare
the way she used to be
look at me, I breathe
is it my grey hair
that makes you dream
drink on glossy evenings
would you care
the nights I spent free
with someone's being
time of certainty with her
fresh at fifty three
blowing like steam
your eyes flared
singing out a scream
what might have been
it's not fair
from a life of ease
you, my new Queen.

Magda

You whisper love
on throwaway 'phones
your ravaged face a moon
an arc of pearl doves
a lifetime learning to moan
fly to those who give
luminous as a sign
above the credit zones
your search to earn
you wear a hooded cowl
like saints show their bones
it massages your soul
is that why you use
linen and eau de cologne
what it makes them lose
what you have above
or in gardens lie prone
beyond police sirens
your star's not alone.

Nika

What you would never do
stuff you swore
ride horses in fields of blue
dance again to the moon
pray to broken laws
like a saddled broom
my partner swoons
what are you saying this for
only fools live out of tune
I want to run away doomed
take holy orders
drain summer into June
rage at every heirloom
divide it by whores
leave you here to stew
a fool to give you room
you lay a heavy score
my almond thighs are ruined
love is raw.

Oriana

Give me demon jewels
and let me laugh through tears
I will dance with fools
under cold white stars
golden gowns stroke my fears
I can't believe this farce
my dreams are for other scenes
citizen comrades brought near
given money to preen
I smile and remember
those ached for years
when there was no pretending
I turn my head, shrug a look
don't want to hear
what she's done
her long gait and twisted cool
this perfume costs me dear
my whole life being cruel
can anyone see clear?

Osta

She says a dawn novena
and worries about her feet
dancing who will see her
love's a trick to trap her
not knowing her own to keep
or equipped for street scenes
every tune makes its mark
bars fuel her sole conceit
blonde singers and wood yards
they rise to greet her
but when morning turns green
she prays untethered
wondering if there is a heaven
more than any depth of need
betting always evens
perhaps with a communion beat
maybe a retreat
she can rescue everything
that makes her dream.

Octavia

Will she dip me now
make me drink more drink
sit and wonder how
her eyes beaten brown
she dances on the brink
this Summer long
the heat off her brow
gathers and sinks
what she might show
like a ship's bow
how she can tinker
or scatter sorrow
constrained I wait near
know what she's thinking
her intentions are clear
I won't need a path
never a shrink
a new lover somehow
time to think.

Ola

Like a swathe of flowers
your lace covered arms
disguise a family ruin
you glide and cruise
does the chemical farm
rock your tunes
creak you like a tower
swing you by the yard arm
stir yellow paint drums
do you brighten, bellow
fugue with alarm
at the absence of glue
a lover here and now
make you feel warm
dance light or blue
rage about your mother
an absence of charm
drugs are your showers
a rain washed calm.

Petra

I walk without fear
down lilac evening
mother's words *hush dear*
wondering what they know
or who they've seen
never bring one to this door
do you remember that photographer
Dada used to tease
looked after, time served
she's in California now
they lived long on our street
houses bought, Protestants
tried to film her father once
Sunday suit, collar at ease
a Carter who swore at her
large hands, still healing
I loved her but was uneasy
kissing by piers
whispering like thieves.

Pilar

Does my hardness mock
your white face, red lips
the sheets you rocked
startled by river song
the sound of ships
Nana use to pummel
then hang out to dry
crowded bars, wine to sip
like geese they cry
cigarette papers unfiled
like Easter lambs who skip
across a crowded sky
are you happy here
in this house of sin
having me lie in them
my Ma boiling socks
making bath house trips
while you sit icon locked
eyes gripped.

Paloma

My time goes by unspoken
afraid of family especially Pa
our farm closed and broken
which hand did you hold
inside the stables pathway glare
sun struck leaves me sore
my days scattered unfold
no one sees my star
or hears a silent roar
that memory won't emote
chime or beat of bell jar
awaken lost Mimosa
steal away like a ghost
elbow grease a foreign bar
have to deal with cuckolds
see the crime as a token
why say *tu voir*
not so easy to let it go
we never travel far.

Patricia

Eyes beat like fireflies
you are no one's fool
they dance like satyrs
jingle like dandelions
this Sunday in June
one side of life
sunlight swathes our ties
you're 28 and cool
it gets you by
track side of trains
the way you move
your lace covered veins
a family's ruin
the money you took
parading your lovers
not poor and righteous
or methadone cruel
it could be Vera Cruz
the way they drool.

Queenie

Can you love me
from your runaway horse
the way she screamed
look at me, I whisper
you've run this way before
do you think I'll resist
what are you doing here
no sorrow or remorse
betting that I'll be free
is this your kingdom
I'm not your whore
of a thousand wishes
I spend time waiting
inside doors
hustle stations for buses, trains
like New York
they know the score
days to kill without a snort
give me more.

Quantilla

If I'm not too late
I'll dance with you
each evening by your gate
swept by your ribbons
melted lemon blue
your yellow hair and whispers
down fallen roads
my mother says only be true
but she doesn't know
your love and mine
our trips to secret venues
flowers smell like wine
I'm lucky in love
no church reason or virtue
your sky sails above
in this time of hate
make me swoon
trust me to say
forget the rumours.

Quamra

Across my forearm lover
my sleeve a chance number
she points to the others
her face a sweet mirror
garett astonished wonder
hearing the whispers
I feel myself crumble
how the world slumbers
at this illicit silver
night winds sing like leather
beyond our daily jumble
they make our days hover
fighting over what is done
fire and distant thunder
why we had to run
one unwashed sign above us
outsiders walk under
some won't make sunset
scattered, sundered.

Rain

On short days she says a blessing
for the drinkers and vagrants
all those others gone missing
on the island there's a mission
behind where cruise ships lay
she makes it her monument
a mind awash with waves
she rushes to this green oasis
departing tourist games
she hears the laughter
sees beach like wraiths
dance beneath sun and madness
belayed by sons and issue
they are not to blame
she skirts around the kissing
makes an unlit confession
feels the convent's sweet glaze
a scented loving admission
touches ancient flame.

Rula

Who brings a lie
to a thirteen year old life
one you can't deny
smoking endless cigarettes
chasing a number why
with the same regrets
the river in May
the cool evening light
when are debts ever paid?
they killed Papa in '38
I danced for Stalin terrified
worried to meet his gaze
Tass reported the scene
it was good for Philliskaya
they tell me see reason
my handsome guys
love measured nights
to dance for the Bolshoi
I see a child.

Rania

Before you turned to me
and carried me with your bite
I knew what it was to be free
what gave you that legitimacy
our love I thought was right
the fire you released
ships fanned for their speed
whispered sails at night
you were my every need
in a sunlit garden at Thebes
a power beyond my sight
you left me solitary
three days I wept inside
whole cities heard me cry
knowing my song denied
wailed out our island creed
don't spare me your delight
like a broken scream
the siren in my smile.

Rabiah

Please don't let them see
why you ring my feet
I only asked for freedom
your consoling love
a village soul and shady tree
here in this crowded boat
I sing to you all of woods
a bitter chant of make believe
in your eyes all that's good
we have coursed with blood
this swarm of human seed
the only thing we could
to smell the wound of Syria
Lesbos and a moonlit sea
broken what we can't retrieve
slave ships know our keening
hands with heavy greeting
shout 'it's time to leave,'
we melt to memory.

Sheila

When you talk coastlines
when you talk rain
what is the cost
don't waste my time
coming home you say
what you think is a lie
smile for the mirror
wait for a dismal train
stand there and shiver
feted by your mantle
a bridge across the plain
your Da lit a candle
for our youngest child
who suffers like a vagrant
behind the cruise lanes
you witness the crime
in Ireland there's a highway
without any signs
it won't ease the pain.

Sophie

Do we keep or burn
a love like gas
the flame turned down
you can demand an urn
now time has passed
not strung out on Meths
Crack not enough
your Da won't collapse
somehow you'll recover
in smoky broken bars
with words so crass
they don't travel far
all I did was write them
to hold you fast
bring you to the tap
let you take your turn
warm your fingers
talk disaster, make you laugh
you never did learn
the word *perhaps*?

Tanya

Don't leave your schemes
with nursing assistants
yearn for lost leanings
that's for blond curls
don't travel that distance
you were never that girl
but a shipwrecked rover
a golden gate sister
paver of those coming after
spreader of resistance
a ridder of injustice
you graced by your stance
how different is midnight
the burden of hospice
angels with white lights
when death lies dreaming
sing 'te deum' banish Christmas
don't expire keening
no one does it for us.

Tomasina

Her day is just beginning
she dances in the tide
fresh and alive and kicking
she kills me with that spin
next to me like a bride
twists her lips like shillings
around a constant cigarette
tobacco blonde full of lies
a dancer not famous yet
like the sea off Burbo Bank
her smile beams estuary wide
arriving where my heart sank
she isn't from Ireland
who never left a family's side
but came here alone
a Medea used to thrilling
a bird made to glide
she can demand anything
sunlight, water, sky.

Una

A crescent moon at Easter
I know I am loved
but want to be free
surrounded by icy streets
I turn my face towards
the gentle mill pond sea
I have reached a breach
Our Lady holds a dove
no matter what she sings
in the cold light of reason
my time is of the trouble
reminds me to the season
by the trees at Freshfield
I dance like a moth
scream a daughter's feelings
a Catholic and a keeper
my Da stands good enough
but cannot give credence
why I act so tough.

Ulana

From starboard you wail to me
'where is the baby'
a terrified moan across the sea
a crescent moon at Christmas
we don't know where to be
the radar off the mast
surrounded by auxiliaries
coastguard lights blink officially
wind hides folded screams
they bring us into Sicily
Our Lady hold her fast
this Garden of broken dreams
no matter what we sing
indifferent or responsibly
someone here knows everything
they have fled the scene
but God will find a way
in the cold light of spring
He'll have his say.

Virginia

More than any laughter
love seeps around her knees
like broken water
inflated or in despair
she can cry when she pleases
if it's absent she cares
but it's not hell
to that other disease
a used cartridge drum knell
she stands by the river
swears she'll never release
the name of that woman
manner of her distance
she knows what she's leaving
a quiet celebration
times in her history
a yellow light of feasting
she dreams of Paris
to do what she feels.

Wyona

Who will tend our bones
how beautiful her kiss
will a river wash the stones
my wrists around her groaning
her body pallid, limpid
lays upon the floor
dying Lupins nod and blow
their faces to the wind
birds sing and sing alone
their song has a flow
of wood pigeons we came across
on Christmas fields unsown
dive down across the moss
babies she missed
her Sunday eyes older
she whispers for a loan
remembers broken missions
smiling before she goes
they fly before the mist.

Wanda

Isn't it good to know
by travel, wine or grounds
when our life is over
will it resist all moaning
wooden planks hold me down
light dancing on the foam
in the luminous flow
you may wonder
what you dream of in going
when you stand by water
sunlight at the ponds
Sunday in late October
how beautiful you are
your lips show the marks
where my passion arcs
and they lower me down
their faces brown
is this is how we know
love's always around?

Xona

Why won't you let me see
please don't bind my feet
I only asked for freedom
consolation of his seed
a human soul or shady tree
beside these heaving beings
I sing you all a canta
a bitter chant of make believe
for your eyes on destiny
as you wait for trains
you swarm of human need
only one song remains
the dancing wound of Syria
Greece and a moonlit sea
rock of Simon Peter
Europe hear my keening
New York light a greeting
boatmen cry 'time to leave'
sail or enter history.

Xaria

Truth was never easy for you
especially on this campaign
your breath warm fish glue
sits frightened on my lips
this no child's game
iron scabbard at the hip
what am I doing being blue
chasing my days
with a woman like you
who cannot be brought
outside of slavery
a sheath of cotton wrought,
around your lies
golden trinket silken delay
all your crass disguise
better to be true
face down outrageous claims
sail by stars to Maputu
Africa on your blade.

Yesna

Our ship enters the bite
they love women dancers here
in darkness and green light
tell me, tell me why
I dream like a seer
my hips dissolve their sighs
I dangle translucent guides
candles scent their fear
when bells ring the night
this boat contains no sleep
yellow rope failed Pirateer
we return from the sea
lurch like Nabateam
through the city streets
dreaming desolate dreams
will they ring my eyes
tell me when I'm clear
beg for more delight
demand to see the tears?

Yerma

She kills me with laughter
on her sunny days
dances like a warrior
talks of a writer
who is bright and unfazed
called Elena Ferrante
who never left her mother
tho' she travelled anyway
a young beat woman
but it brings me no surprise
hearing the midnight train
when love bids good night
the soul of my being
kisses like the rain
on St Bartholomew's quay
that sense of wonder
morning café strange
the pain of daughters'
across my face.

Yaya

Separate us from our best
find a sail to make us shrill
our fight to change address
a raging thirst we can't refresh
a map, some salt, make us kill
a hope we can't address
if there is more to caress
battered nights leave us still
fix our weathered compass
locate the hungry west
let us eat our fill
hope we pass the test
shape our days at sea or rest
face each wave and rill
struggle each duress
send us back if we egress
devoured by men or kids
by flames or water to confess
we can take the pill.

Yanka

How do I take this scene
looking sweet on vodka
as if it will protect me
off my face with anxiety
mascara pushed down the sofa
eyes looking furtively
fix this place like a firefly
red and yellow dank cellar
her fingers wave Hi
my greatest days contained
she loosens first my collar
we sit side by side restrained
she is like a gift from the sea
she brings me *Rioja*
at the next epiphany
doesn't bother with history
has neither sou nor dollar
explores my territory
no one here to stop her.

Zita

What I was feeling then
can't be undone
I won't see you again
when you sent me reeling
dancing forlorn
where else but the sea
freedom is a sense of being
unlike Anthony Powell
who'd given a son to school
then sat unfeeling
to drive home alone
I couldn't dream of Pliny
or pray on my knees
turning to the stones
mine was never to please
so sister let me suggest
when our path is done
use lipstick to redress
the river for your pen.

Biographical Note

Molly Smyth was born in Belfast in 1931 and brought to Liverpool aged two months from an orphanage in Ireland. Her mother Ginny Smyth (nee Murphy) had a sister, one of thirteen, who worked there and helped despatch unwanted children to Liverpool and American families. Molly was the last of six brought across the Irish Sea. Ginny Smyth used to prepare for her own 'trips' by steadily adding cushions to her waistline before the departure of 'the cattle boat' from the Princes dock.

Molly's father, John Smyth, a cooper from the 'Liberties' in Dublin had settled in Liverpool in 1905 and worked at the Bank Hall cooperage in the North End of the city. He was present in the 'second wave' of the general transport strike that gripped Liverpool in the boiling summer of 1911 and which led to the organisation of the casual trades all along the seven miles of the City's waterfront.

He died in 1935 leaving the family a rich cultural legacy but little in the way of money, swallowed by his lengthy bronchial condition. Poorly provided for, Molly's brothers went to sea and her sisters worked at factories in and around the docks.

Always being of an independent nature, a bit of a rebel, the youngest and spoiled especially when her brothers came home, Molly was a great dancer. She followed her sisters up and down the parishes and clubs of Bootle, Seaforth and Waterloo and then left Liverpool in 1950 to go and work in London. She had trained as a secretary, paid for by her brothers' allotment notes and by her mother's obduracy and was provided 'with something more than just tapping her feet'. Being the youngest, she was allowed to make her way. For the next forty years she lived and worked between Camden Town, Victoria and Hackney, 'a lifetime between the 24 and the 38 bus routes' she once said.

In 1963 she married the photographer Antonio Lorrazzi. It wasn't conventional. They had three children together over the next ten years. Lonely when she first arrived in London she embarked upon the extra mural programmes provided by Birkbeck College. She met friends there amongst women that were to last a lifetime. Throughout this time she continued with her dancing whilst holding down day jobs as secretarial support in offices.

At the age of 35 and with her first child a toddler (Peter Constantine) she took up an appointment as a low level clerk within the portals of the Home Office where she had been working casually since her son was born. She stayed there for twenty five years and rose steadily through the secretarial system to confirm the security her mother had craved, aided and abetted by increasingly progressive laws for working women within the civil service. But she never stopped dancing and going out. She loved her holidays in Spain.

Her husband turned increasingly to drink after the failure of his business and after a third child, a daughter Patricia, was born in 1973. The photography had started to diminish some years before this and the marriage became increasingly fraught with bitter episodes. This was not helped by Molly's increasingly open sexual intimacy with women from her college and dancing days.

Ten years later, she relinquished all rights to the house in Camden when she chose to live with her long time partner Sandra Gluckman in a communal house in Hackney. The children slowly followed her but made sure their father was looked after in his ailing years. They also were regular visitors to Liverpool when Molly returned alone some eight years later to care for her last sister who was dying of cancer. They remained in the metropolis to minister to their increasingly ill father, Molly stayed.

From an outline of this sparse history it would seem that Molly's richest life was spent on the outside, family, work, lovers, dancing. Apart from the Birkbeck short courses there is little trace of any formal education. Her large circle of friends would indicate a life lived in cafés, in kitchen parties, on dance floors in that quasi bohemian/suburban life many women are lucky enough or dread to live by - something that Molly was well aware.

Yet we have the poems. Throughout her life Molly never offered any of these for publication or sale. Her method of distribution was to post them to friends and relatives – often collected together on Home Office paper which made her laugh. There was never any danger of public recognition although she did once win a bronze medal from the International Library of poetry for the poem 'Blue'.

But the poems are important because of their almost prosaic frugality, the constant evocation of spoken rhythm and colloquialism – her frank and just treatment of sexual persuasion recognising both bohemian and suburban realities combined with her often esoteric but brilliantly alive sense of the modern; the sheer enjoyment of a cosmopolitan existence with a Liverpudlian sense of being.

Molly Smyth came from the working class and in many ways never left it but hers is not an epic of suffering and collective struggle but one of personal decision and unwavering hope. Her laughter rings along the lines of these pages in this her second collection. Its lines reflect the laughter etched into her face and deep in those twinkling brown eyes. She loved a good argument as she did a drink and, of course, the eternal cigarette.

Molly died in January 2014 of the same cancer that afflicted all of her family. 'It just came for me later like a holy wind,' she chuckled and laughed in a haze of blue smoke. She did not really recover after a bout of 'flu in the autumn of the previous year but stayed quietly at home in the North End of the city that she loved so much. She spent her last weeks at a Catholic hospice not far from where the Mersey joins Liverpool Bay, looking out over the woods and big maritime skies. She took communion there each week until the day of her death.

Joan French 2016.

Co Loa Media

Thank you for reading *North End Shore*, we hope you enjoyed it. A review on Amazon would be much appreciated.

Our first Molly Smyth book, *Lovers, Ciggies and a Decastitch* is now available as an ebook from Amazon, details of this and other titles appear on the following pages.

Further details and links to the books on Amazon appear on **www.coloamedia.com**.

Look out for our first Chinese translation in autumn 2017 of 'Behind the Pupil', a short story by Lin, known in China for her books on the exploits of Detective Gao Yi.

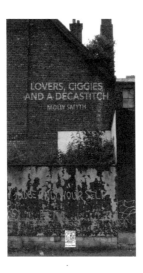

Lovers, Ciggies and a Decastitch
Molly Smyth

I found this book near to Highgate station and loved it.
The ten line poems were great and I could read them
easily on my way to work. They are deceptively simple
but they stay with you. There were parts that read like
Anna Amacktova and others like Carly Simon. This is a
great little book and I would encourage others to read
it.
Amazon review of the paperback edition.

Now available as an ebook from Amazon for £1.99.
112 pages, published March 2017.

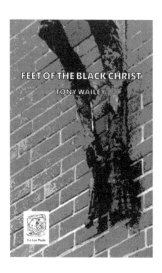

Feet of the Black Christ
Tony Wailey

A wonderful book about a Liverpool family. Coming
from a city of film makers in Italy this Kindle book told
me more about the city than a tour guide. By the time I
had finished I was ready to visit. What a joy to see the
re-installation of the Black Christ on Princes Avenue.
I would urge you to read this book. Guiliana
Amazon review

Available as an ebook from Amazon for £1.15
215 pages, published April 2014

Edgy Cities
Steve Higginson and Tony Wailey

Port cities are different. The bigger the port the bigger the difference. Being located on the edge of the Nation State, they have always been arenas of dissenting cultural expression.

These stories are based upon Time, Memory and Movement and aim to explore the rhythmic pulse from Liverpool to its southernmost European and wider Atlantic horizons.

Available as an ebook from Amazon for 99p
72 pages, published September 2014

The Irish Sea
Tony Wailey

The Irish Sea consists of three long poems, regarding the snooker player Alex Higgins, the footballer George Best and the boxer Johnny Caldwell. All died of drink; all died in poverty either relative or acute. All came from one city and all gained fame in another country.

Available as an ebook from Amazon for 99p
32 pages, published April 2014